Mysterious Encounters

Werewolves

by Kris Hirschmann

KIDHAVEN PRESS

An imprint of Thomson Gale, a part of The Thomson Corporation

THOMSON

GALE

Detroit • New York • San Francisco • San Diego • New Haven, Conn. • Waterville, Maine • London • Munich

Chapter 1

From Man to Beast

Many horror movies show men and women changing into wolves. These frightening creatures, called **werewolves**, were not invented by Hollywood screenwriters, however. They are based on stories and legends that have been told for thousands of years. Since the earliest recorded times, people have believed that werewolves roam the Earth.

What Is a Werewolf?

In legend, a werewolf is a person who can change back and forth between wolf and human forms. Sometimes he or she does this willingly. For instance, a person might switch forms by wearing a magical belt or the skin of a wolf. He or she might also rub a special ointment onto the body, recite a spell, or sometimes both. In most cases a person has to make a pact with the devil before any of these methods will work.

Actor Lon Chaney appears in the 1941 film *The Wolf Man*. Werewolf legends have fascinated us for centuries.

Other stories tell of people who become werewolves unknowingly. This can happen if a person accidentally drinks from certain streams or from rainwater pooled in a wolf's paw prints. The full moon can bring on a werewolf **transformation**. Being bitten by a werewolf is another surefire way to become a werewolf. All of these changes take place whether or not a person wants them.

Legends disagree not only about the transformation process, but also about the final form of the werewolf. Some accounts say that werewolves have some wolf features and some human features. Others say that werewolves look almost like real wolves. They are much larger and fiercer, though, and there is usually something oddly human about their eyes.

In legend, the personalities of werewolves vary. Some werewolves talk and think just like their human selves. They are friendly, refined, and helpful. Others start thinking like wolves as soon as they transform. These werewolves are likely to lose control of themselves. They are extremely vicious and will not hesitate to kill any human who gets in their way.

The History of Werewolves

The earliest legendary werewolf may have been Lycaon. Lycaon was a mythological Greek king who served roasted human flesh to the god Zeus. Furious at this insult, Zeus changed Lycaon into a wolf.

In a Greek myth, Zeus changes King Lycaon into a wolf as punishment for serving him a meal of human flesh.

Since the days of Greek mythology, werewolf stories have emerged in practically every culture around the world. Many of these stories take the form of fairy tales. One popular tale has been told over and over again in slightly different ways by the brothers Grimm and others. The story goes something like this: A man is hunting in the woods when he is attacked by a wolf. The wolf is enormous and ferocious, and it seems determined to kill the man. Luckily, the man is big and strong. He manages to pull out his knife. With one mighty swipe, he cuts off the wolf's right front paw.

The wolf yelps and limps away into the forest. The shaken hunter returns home. He is eager to tell his wife about what has happened. But upon entering the house, the man finds his wife disheveled, blood-streaked, and crying. She holds out her right arm, revealing only a stump where her hand used to be.

Tales like this were probably based on so-called real-life werewolf encounters. In other words, they

Werewolf Diseases

A disease called porphyria makes the teeth red and may cause its victims to howl like dogs. People with a disease called hypertrichosis are born with long hair covering their bodies. Conditions like these may account for some long-ago werewolves.

This 1909 illustration depicts a young man thought to suffer from hypertrichosis.

originally came from people who really believed they had seen or been attacked by werewolves.

Overrun with Werewolves

Belief in werewolves was particularly strong in the 1500s and 1600s. At this time some European countries, especially France, seem to have been overrun with the beasts. Legal records show that up to 30,000 people were accused of being werewolves during this era, and many were executed for their supposed crimes.

Today, the idea of trying someone for werewolvery seems ridiculous. But centuries ago, the idea did not seem so silly. There was no question then about whether werewolves were real; everyone was certain that they were. Of course, there were disagreements about exactly how people became werewolves and how they changed form. There was even some debate about whether werewolves actually transformed or whether they were just enchanted by the devil so that both the werewolf and other people perceived a change. But few people doubted that werewolves did exist.

During this period, many people confessed to being werewolves. Undoubtedly most of them really believed it. Many other people claimed to have had encounters with werewolves, and undoubtedly they really believed it, too. With so much apparent proof, it is no wonder people everywhere accepted werewolves as a fact of life.

Are Werewolves Real?

Times have changed since the **heyday** of the werewolf. Today, most people do not believe in magical creatures. They do not think that werewolves exist, or that they have ever existed.

But some people disagree. Even in modern times, a surprising number of werewolf sightings have occurred. Most people do not report these sightings because they are afraid they will be laughed at. But when given the chance, werewolf victims are happy to share their experiences without leaving their names. In 1988 the Fox television network ran a "Werewolf Hotline" that people could dial if they thought they had seen a werewolf. The hotline logged hundreds of thousands of calls in the short time it was open.

People today do not just see werewolves. Some people even continue to claim they are werewolves. Few modern werewolves believe that a physical change takes place. They think the shift from human to wolf form is mental or spiritual. But they are firmly convinced that they do experience a transformation when the moon is full. "We aren't roleplayers, jokesters, or pretenders. We really do believe it," explains one self-professed werewolf. "Just because [the shift] is somewhat symbolic . . . doesn't mean that it is just pretend or a game. It is very real and serious business."[1]

A very few modern werewolves say their bodies actually change shape. These people are usually

In this fanciful picture, werewolves howl at the moon. Some people believe humans transform into werewolves during a full moon.

considered to be mentally ill. Even many spiritual werewolves do not believe the claims of the shape-shifters. But disbelief does not necessarily make something untrue. Who knows? Maybe humans-turned-wolf do, indeed, roam today's cities and countrysides under the eerie light of the full moon.

Chapter 2

Werewolf Sightings

In July 1958, a Texas woman named Mrs. Delburt Gregg was settling down for a good night's rest. The evening was hot, so Gregg pulled her bed close to a screened window. She hoped to catch a breeze from a thunderstorm that was brewing in the distance.

Having moved her bed, Gregg hopped in and dozed off. A short time later, she was awakened by a scratching sound on the screen. At that moment lightning flashed, revealing a "huge, shaggy, wolflike creature . . . clawing at the screen and glaring at me with baleful, glowing, slitted eyes. I could see its bared white fangs."[2]

Gregg watched, terrified, as the creature ran across her yard and dove into a group of bushes. Gregg waited for the beast to reappear on the other side, but "instead of a great shaggy wolf running out, the figure of an extremely tall man suddenly parted the thick foliage and walked hurriedly down the road, disappearing into the darkness."[3]

Werewolf literature is full of accounts like this. From ancient days all the way through modern times, people have reported seeing mysterious creatures that look and act like werewolves.

Werewolves terrify their victims by baring their fangs and growling like enraged animals.

Half Asleep

A person who has been startled out of a deep sleep is not usually thinking very clearly. For a short time, he or she might even think dream images are real. This fact might explain Mrs. Delburt Gregg's alleged werewolf sighting.

People just waking from sleep often have trouble seeing things clearly. Images they think are real may be left over from dreams.

Ghostly Werewolf

One especially creepy werewolf story comes from the writings of Elliott O'Donnell, an English researcher who lived and worked in the late 1800s and early 1900s. O'Donnell interviewed a woman he identified as Miss St. Denis. This young woman sketched as a hobby, and she often worked at a sleepy local train station with a good view of the surrounding neighborhood. Usually St. Denis left the station well before dark. But one day, caught up in her work, she found herself on the platform as night was beginning to fall. Looking up with a start, St. Denis noticed someone nearby, watching her.

The figure sat still and silent. St. Denis coughed once, and then again, hoping to get a response. But there was none. "Can you tell me the time, please?"[4] she asked. When the figure still did not respond, St. Denis became nervous. She gathered her things and briskly walked away. After going a short distance, St. Denis glanced back over her shoulder— and discovered she was being followed.

St. Denis knew she was in a bad situation. The road was deserted and nearly pitch black. If the stranger attacked, St. Denis had very little chance of getting anyone's attention. Her only chance, she figured, was to confront her stalker. So, screwing up her courage, St. Denis swung around and raised herself to her full height. "What do you want? How dare you?" she cried. O'Donnell describes what happened next:

She got no further, for a sudden spurt of dying sunlight, playing over the figure, showed her it was nothing human, nothing she had ever conceived possible. It was a nude grey thing, not unlike a man in body, but with a wolf's head. As it sprang forward, its light eyes ablaze with ferocity, [St. Denis] instinctively felt in her pocket, whipped out a pocket flashlight, and pressed the button. The effect was magical; the creature shrank back, and putting two paw-like hands in front of its face to protect its eyes, faded into nothingness.[5]

Following this frightening incident, St. Denis made inquiries about what she had seen. She learned that some odd bones—part human, part animal—had been found near the train station. Based on this information, St. Denis concluded that she had probably seen the ghost of a werewolf.

The Gallup Wolf

Less creepy, but equally odd, is the report of a 1970 werewolf sighting near Gallup, New Mexico. Four young men were driving just outside town when a hairy two-legged beast appeared next to their car. Although the car was traveling at 45 miles (72k) per hour, the creature had no trouble keeping up. The driver, Clifford Heronemus, sped up to 60 miles (97k) per hour, but still the wolf-like creature kept up with the car.

At this point Heronemus and his passengers became very frightened. The road on which they were driving was full of sharp turns. If the car skidded off the road, the four friends would be easy pickings for the monster. Before this could happen, however, one of the passengers pulled out a gun and shot at the beast. "I know it got hit and it fell down—but there was no blood. It got up again and ran off,"[6] Heronemus said later.

It is impossible to say for sure what the young men saw that night. But Heronemus is positive it was not a human being. "I know it couldn't have been a person, because people cannot move that fast,"[7] he says. He and his friends are convinced that the creature outside the car was a werewolf.

Werewolves are said to have sharp fangs that are very different from human teeth.

The Bray Road Beast

A werewolf may have been behind a series of odd sightings in southeastern Wisconsin as well. The first report of the "Bray Road Beast," as the creature was eventually dubbed, occurred on October 31, 1999.

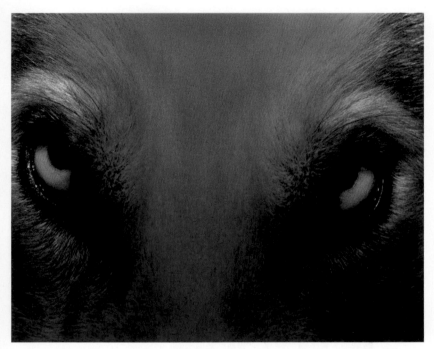

Some werewolves are described as having glowing yellow eyes that reflect light.

A young woman named Doristine Gipson was driving along Bray Road near the town of Delavan when she felt her car jerk as if she had hit something. Gipson stopped the car and got out to see what had happened. She did not see anything beneath her car—but when she looked around, she saw a dark, hairy figure racing toward her. Gipson threw herself back into the car and slammed the door. As she tried to drive away, the creature leaped onto her trunk. The trunk was wet and slippery, though, and the creature fell off.

Word soon spread about Gipson's frightening experience. As it did, more people came forward to share similar sightings. One of these accounts came from a woman named Lorianne Endrizzi. In 1989 Endrizzi was driving down Bray Road when she saw what she thought was a man kneeling at the side of the road. She slowed down to see if the man was hurt. But what she saw was not a human at all. It was a wolf-like creature that Endrizzi later described as having grayish-brown hair, fangs, and pointed ears. Furthermore, she said, "His face was . . . long and snouty, like a wolf."[8] She also noticed that the creature's eyes were glowing a sickly yellow, as animals' eyes do when they reflect light.

In a later interview, Endrizzi said that the creature "appeared to be so human-like that it was scary."[9] At the time of the incident, she said, she had no idea what she had seen. But later she saw a book that contained an illustration of a werewolf. The resemblance was incredible. From that moment on, Endrizzi was sure she had seen a werewolf lurking along Bray Road.

What Is the Bray Road Beast?

Following these two reports, many other locals stepped forward with stories of an unusual creature. Most of the encounters took place between 1989 and 1992, but the beast was occasionally seen long past that period. The most recent incident occurred on March 9, 2005, when a University of Wisconsin student saw a shaggy 6-foot-tall (1.8m) figure striding across a local highway. In all, about 50 people claim to have seen the creature.

Skeptics argue that werewolf sightings are actually encounters with real wolves like this one.

So what is the Bray Road Beast? Skeptics say
it may be a coyote, a regular wolf, a bear, or per-
haps a wolf/dog mix. But believers say there is
no way it could be any of these things. "Do we
dare consider the idea that the beast was a shapeshifter of some sort, blending between man and
wolf?"[10] asks author and **paranormal** investigator Troy Taylor. Most people will never accept
this view. But to those who have seen this bizarre
creature in action, Taylor's explanation may be
the only one that makes sense.

Chapter 3

Werewolf Attacks

According to legend, werewolves can be perfectly pleasant when they are in human form. When they transform into wolves, however, these same individuals may become angry and ferocious. There are many accounts, almost all from long-ago times, of werewolves attacking and even killing human victims.

The Beast of Gévaudan

History's most famous werewolf is undoubtedly the Beast of Gévaudan. This bloodthirsty creature roamed the Auvergne and South Dordogne regions of France between 1764 and 1767. During its reign of terror, the beast—known in France simply as "La Bête"—killed about 100 people.

The beast's first attack occurred in July 1764. A young girl went out one morning to tend a flock of sheep and did not return. When the townspeople went looking for the girl, they found her body in a valley with her heart torn out. Over the next few days, several more children were found in a similar state.

"La Bête Is No Wolf"

These incidents threw the region into a panic. The panic turned out to be well founded, because the beast's attacks continued over the next few years. The attacks were so vicious that people started to believe no normal animal could be responsible. Even the authorities agreed. "La Bête is no wolf,"[11] announced one 18th-century wolf expert. Word spread that the beast must be a **loup-garou** (the French word for werewolf).

A few people encountered the beast and lived to tell the tale. In one case, a farmer was out cutting his wheat when he saw a movement nearby. Seconds later, the beast emerged from the depths of the wheat field and bounded toward the man. The farmer managed to fight off the creature by swinging his **scythe**, but he was so terrified that he was unable to speak for hours afterward.

Another story tells of a young mother named Jeanne Jouve who was walking with three of her children when the beast attacked. Using only rocks and her bare hands, Jouve struggled with the monster. Eventually the beast retreated, but it left Jouve seriously injured and one child dead.

This illustration depicts the Beast of Gévaudan attacking a young woman.

What Was the Beast?

Various modern scholars say that the Beast of Gévaudan was a wolf/dog mix, some kind of big cat, a surviving prehistoric creature, or even an alien. Few believe it was an actual werewolf.

The Beast of Gévaudan attacked numerous children during the three years it terrorized France.

The attacks continued until June 1767, when a local nobleman organized a party of hunters to track down and destroy the beast once and for all. After a long hunt, the creature was finally found. It was brought down by a hunter named Jean Chastel, whose gun was loaded with silver bullets. According to some legends, only silver could kill werewolves.

The Welsh Werewolf

About twenty years after the Beast of Gévaudan was shot, rumors arose of a werewolf stalking the Welsh countryside. The creature was first sighted in 1790. A stagecoach was traveling along a deserted road when a huge wolf-like animal leaped from the woods. The beast attacked and overturned the stagecoach, then turned its attention to the terrified horses. One horse managed to break its harness and escape into the night. The other horse, trapped and helpless, was quickly killed by the mysterious creature.

The beast was not seen for a while, but it resurfaced in the winter of 1791. One chilly night, a man noticed enormous paw prints in the snow. He and the local blacksmith followed the prints to a nearby field, where they made a gory discovery. The snowy pasture was red with blood, and it was dotted with the dead bodies of sheep, cattle, and even a dog.

Having witnessed this terrible scene, the man and the blacksmith became concerned about the farmer who owned the bloody field. They rushed to the farmer's house and found the man inside, shaking with fear. When questioned, the farmer said he had come upon a huge, black, wolf-like animal attacking his sheepdog. The animal had turned and run toward the farmer, but the man was able to get into his house and slammed the door before the creature could attack. Author and paranormal investigator Tom Slemen describes what happened next:

> The wolf pounded on the heavy oak door, almost knocking it off its hinges. The weird-looking animal then stood up on its hind legs like a human and looked in through the windows of the farmhouse. Its eyes were blue and seemed intelligent and almost human-like. The beast foamed at the mouth as it peered in, then bolted from the window to commit carnage on the farm.[12]

The following day, church officials announced that the creature must have been a werewolf. Patrols were organized to hunt and kill the beast. But although the villagers looked long and hard, they could not find the deadly animal. Its snowy tracks were the only sign it had ever existed.

Peeter Stubbe

The Welsh werewolf was a mystery and remains so to this day. Another famous werewolf, however, was definitely human—at least part of the time. The werewolf in question went by the name of Peeter Stubbe. This man lived in the late 1500s in a small German town.

A huge beast known as the Welsh werewolf repeatedly attacked sheep and other animals during the 1790s.

According to one historic document, Stubbe asked the devil for the power to work evil on men, women, and children. In response, the document says,

> The Devil . . . gave unto him a girdle [strap] which, being put around him, he was straight transformed into the likeness of a greedy, devouring wolf, strong and mighty, with eyes great and large, which in the night sparkled like unto brands of fire, a mouth great and wide, with most sharp and cruel teeth, a huge body and mighty paws.[13]

Supposedly in wolf form, Stubbe attacked and killed unknown numbers of men, women, and

This woodcut depicts people hunting a werewolf. Villagers often organized hunting expeditions to kill the beasts that terrorized their towns.

According to legend, the devil, depicted here as a dark angel, granted Peeter Stubbe the ability to transform into a werewolf.

children over the next 25 years. If he could not find human victims, he killed sheep, goats, and other livestock.

One account tells of a group of children who narrowly escaped the wolf man. The children were playing in a field when "among these children comes this vile wolf running and caught a pretty fine girl by the collar, with intent to pull out her throat."[14] But the girl's collar was stiff, and the wolf could not bite through it. Meanwhile the cows in the field, protecting their calves, lowered their horns and charged at the beast. The creature released his intended victim and ran away, leaving the child unharmed.

After decades of deaths and near deaths, the townspeople were on the lookout for unusual animals.

In 1589, they found one. As the story goes, a group of men and dogs cornered a huge wolf that was actually Peeter Stubbe in disguise. Realizing that he was trapped, Stubbe slipped off his demonic strap and changed back into a human. The hunters saw this transformation and recognized Stubbe for what he really was—a werewolf. Stubbe was immediately taken into custody and tried for werewolvery. The man proudly admitted to everything of which he was accused, including the murder of his own son. A few days later, he was executed for his crimes.

The Wolf Man of Ohio

No modern-day werewolf stories match the horror and violence of these long-ago tales. Werewolf attacks are still reported—according to one source, there were 23 such reports in 2002 alone—but they are almost always dismissed without investigation or media attention. Police believe that most of the people who come forward with these accounts are making them up.

One of the very few modern stories, which may have a kernel of truth, comes from 1972. A wolf-like figure was spotted several times in Defiance, Ohio. The creature walked upright and, according to Tom Jones, who spotted the beast one moonlit night, "had huge hairy feet, fangs, and ran from side to side, like a caveman in the movies. . . . At first I thought the whole thing was a big joke, but when I saw how hairy and woolly it was, that was enough for me."[15]

This sixteenth-century woodcut presents the story of Peeter Stubbe. As a werewolf Stubbe attacked numerous residents of a German town before being captured, tortured, and finally executed.

Jones saw the creature again a few nights later, at which point the wolf man struck him on the shoulder with a piece of lumber.

Jones was convinced that a werewolf was responsible for this attack. The local police chief, on the other hand, said the attacker was probably a person wearing a wolf mask. It certainly seems unlikely that an actual werewolf would use a wooden club. But this did not stop people from believing that a deadly and supernatural animal was roaming the streets of Defiance. Until the sightings stopped, doors were slammed, locked, and bolted tight—just as they have always been against the coming of the wolf.

Chapter 4

The Wolf Madness

In long-ago times, the word **lycanthrope** meant the same thing as werewolf. Today, the word has a deeper meaning. It refers to people who truly believe they change into werewolves, even when no change is apparent to an observer. This belief is called **lycanthropy**, and it is generally considered a mental illness.

People have suffered from lycanthropy throughout recorded history. There are many accounts, both historic and modern, of encounters with these wolves of the mind.

A Werewolf Family

Records show that an entire family of lycanthropes, the Gandillons, lived in France in the late 1500s.

Treating Lycanthropy

Lycanthropes take special **psychoactive** drugs to cure their illness. These drugs fix the chemical problems in the brain that lead to lycanthropy.

People who suffer from the mental illness lycanthropy truly believe that they transform into werewolves.

The disorder was especially strong in a woman named Pernette. It was Pernette's habit to roam the countryside on her hands and knees, filthy and howling like a wolf. One day in 1598, Pernette came across a young brother and sister when she was in

This illustration shows a man behaving like a beast. Lycanthropes mimic wolf-like movements by crawling on their hands and feet.

this condition. She attacked the little girl, evidently meaning to kill and eat her. But the girl's brother pulled out a knife and began to defend his sister. Enraged, Pernette snatched the knife and stabbed the brother, who later died of his wounds. Pernette was captured and put to death following this incident.

Special Ointment

Soon afterward, attention turned to Pernette's brother, Pierre. Pierre was accused of having smeared himself with a special ointment that let him "run about the country in the form of a wolf." The accused man was happy to confess to these charges. He also told authorities that "he had, during the period of his transformation, fallen on, and devoured, both beasts and human beings."[16] Pierre's son, Georges, later confessed that he, too, was a werewolf and had attacked two goats while in his wolf state.

Pierre and Georges were thrown into prison. In their cells, the two men behaved like maniacs, scampering around on all fours and howling. Observers noticed that the prisoners' bodies were covered with scars, probably because dogs had attacked the men during their werewolf ramblings.

The two lycanthropes did not change into wolves while they were imprisoned. But this fact was not considered important. Authorities reasoned that Pierre and Georges did not have the special ointment they needed, so of course they would not be able to transform themselves in jail.

They were werewolves nonetheless. Pierre and Georges were hanged for their terrible crimes and then burned as well, just for good measure.

Jean Grenier

Just a few years later, in 1603, another lycanthrope was discovered in southern France. The case began when a thirteen-year-old girl named Marguerite Poirier came forward with a frightening tale. She usually tended her parents' sheep along with a young man named Jean Grenier, who often terrified her with stories about changing into a wolf.

One day Jean wandered off. Soon afterward some bushes near Marguerite began to shake. Marguerite thought Jean was returning—but instead a red-haired, wolf-like beast leaped out of the bushes and rushed toward the girl. The animal used its sharp fangs to rip Marguerite's clothes and scratch her body. Before the creature could do more damage, Marguerite fought it off with her shepherd's staff.

After this incident, Marguerite rushed home and told her parents what had happened. She was convinced that her attacker had been Jean Grenier in animal form. Based on Marguerite's story, the local authorities took Jean into custody. They questioned the young man, who admitted that he had been responsible for the attack. "The charge of Marguerite Poirier is correct. My intention was to have killed and devoured her, but she kept me off with a stick," he said. Jean further explained that

when he was ten or eleven years old, a man had given him a special **salve** and a wolf skin, and "from that time I have run about the country as a wolf."[17]

Jean claimed that he had killed and eaten many children while he was in wolf form. He provided dates and locations for all of these crimes. Authorities checked Jean's information and found that children had indeed gone missing from the areas mentioned on the dates Jean gave. It is therefore likely that Jean really did do the terrible things he said he did.

It was not certain, however, that he did them in the shape of a wolf. Despite Marguerite's story, the evidence suggested that Jean only thought he could turn into an animal. Members of the court decided

This scene from the 2002 movie *Dog Soldiers* shows a werewolf hunting for prey in the forest.

that Jean was not in league with the devil, he was only insane. So instead of sentencing the young man to death, they sent him to a monastery. Jean lived in the monastery for seven years, acting more and more wolf-like as the years passed and his madness deepened. He died at the age of twenty, still vowing that he would continue chasing and eating children if only he were free.

A Modern-Day Werewolf

Mental health professionals sometimes discover lycanthropes even today. One well-documented modern case involves Bill Ramsey, whose tale was told in a 1991 book. Ramsey first felt the werewolf change when he was nine years old. He was playing in his backyard when he felt a coldness come over him. He began to feel furious for no reason, and images of himself as a wolf flashed through his mind. His terrified parents watched their son uproot a fence post and destroy part of the fence with his teeth before the episode finally ended.

Ramsey experienced several other werewolf "shifts" during his lifetime. The best eyewitness account comes from an incident that happened when Ramsey was an adult. It started when a terrified woman approached a police officer named Terry Fisher and asked him to protect her from a frightening stranger. When Fisher went outside to investigate, he got his first glimpse of Ramsey. He explains what happened next:

He just watched me. . . . There was something not quite human in the eyes, particularly. For the first time, I started to feel a little nervous. . . . A kind of low rumbling started up in his chest and rose to his throat. At first, I thought I'd confused this with one of the dogs growling. Then I realized it was Bill Ramsey. . . . Before I knew what was happening, he threw me to the ground and got on top of me. His face underwent an incredible transformation. His eyes got especially crazy. His lip pulled back over his teeth and his hands suddenly became claw-like. He was tearing at me the way an animal would, as if he was trying to rend my flesh.[18]

Fisher survived his encounter with Ramsey, who later claimed he was possessed by a demon. After hearing this claim, a Roman Catholic bishop offered to perform an **exorcism** on Ramsey. The exorcism worked. The demon was forced out of Ramsey's body, and the man's werewolf troubles at long last were over.

This story can be viewed in different ways. Many people believe that Ramsey was actually possessed by an evil spirit. Others think he was suffering from a severe form of lycanthropy. Ramsey was cured by the exorcism because he truly believed the demon had been ripped from his body. This belief was strong enough to end his werewolf episodes for good.

This painting portrays an exorcism during the 1500s. Exorcisms have been performed on lycanthropes throughout history.

There is no way to say for sure what really happened to Bill Ramsey. But as in all werewolf cases, public opinions vary. Most people are skeptical. Some, however, are fully convinced. As long as werewolf sightings and attacks occur, there will always be people who believe that these bloodthirsty creatures howl and prowl whenever the moon is full.

Notes

Chapter 1: From Man to Beast

1. The Werewolf and Shapeshifter Codex, "FAQ for Humans Who Want to Know About Shifters," http://yaiolani.tripod.com/humfaq.htm.

Chapter 2: Werewolf Sightings

2. Mrs. Delburt Gregg, "True Mystic Experiences: Werewolf?" *Fate*, March 1960, pp. 60.

3. Gregg, "True Mystic Experiences: Werewolf?" pp. 60.

4. Quoted in Elliott O'Donnell, *British Werewolves*, 1914. HorrorMasters, www.horrormasters.com/Themes/Werewolves.htm.

5. O'Donnell, *British Werewolves*.

6. Quoted in John W. Whitehead, "Under the Full Moon: Werewolf Cinema," The Rutherford Institute, October 25, 2004, www.rutherford.org/articles_db/commentary.asp?record_id=305.

7. Quoted in Whitehead, "Under the Full Moon: Werewolf Cinema."

8. Quoted in Troy Taylor, "The Bray Road Beast," Ghosts of the Prairie, 2002, www.prairieghosts.com/brayrd.html.

9. Quoted in Taylor, "The Bray Road Beast."
10. Taylor, "The Bray Road Beast."

Chapter 3: Werewolf Attacks

11. Quoted in Derek Brockis, "What Was the Beast of Gévaudan?" La Bête du Gévaudan, http://labete.7hunters.net/betel.htm.
12. Quoted in Tom Slemen, "Werewolves," BBC Online, 1998, http://www.bbc.co.uk/wales/northeast/guides/weird/mythsandlegends/pages/werewolf.shtml.
13. Quoted in Montague Summers, *The Werewolf.* New York: E.P. Dutton, 1934.
14. Quoted in Summers, *The Werewolf.*
15. Quoted in James Stegall, "Werewolf Case in Defiance Not Viewed Lightly by Police," *Blade*, August 2, 1972. Quoted in News of the Strange, www.geocities.com/zoomarl/wolfman.html.

Chapter 4: The Wolf Madness

16. Quoted in Sabine Baring-Gould, *The Book of Were-Wolves*, 1865, The Internet Sacred Text Archive, www.sacred-texts.com/goth/bow.
17. Quoted in Baring-Gould, *The Book of Were-Wolves.*
18. Quoted in Ed Warren and Lorraine Warren with William Ramsey and Robert David Chase, *Werewolf: A True Story of Demonic Possession.* New York: St. Martin's Press, 1991.

Glossary

exorcism: A ritual designed to banish evil spirits.

heyday: The most active or important period.

hypertrichosis: A disease that causes its victims to grow thick hair over most of their bodies.

loup-garou: The French word for werewolf.

lycanthrope: In the past, this word meant the same thing as werewolf. Today, it means a person who believes he or she is a werewolf.

lycanthropy: The condition of being a lycanthrope, or believing one is a werewolf. Lycanthropy is usually considered a mental illness.

paranormal: Supernatural or not scientifically explainable.

porphyria: A disease with werewolf-like symptoms. Porphyria victims may exhibit sensitive eyes and skin, pale skin, sores, reddish teeth, and animal-like behavior.

psychoactive: Affecting the mind or behavior.

salve: A lotion or ointment that is meant to be rubbed onto the skin.

scythe: A sharp, curved blade attached to a long stick. This tool is designed to cut hay and other crops.

transformation: A dramatic change from one form to another.

werewolves: People who change back and forth between human and wolf form.

For Further Exploration

Books

Toney Allman, *Werewolves*. San Diego, CA: Kid-Haven Press, 2004. This book takes a broad look at werewolves in fact and fiction. It includes sections on possible explanations for werewolf sightings and movie werewolves.

Laura Buller, *Myths and Monsters: From Dragons to Werewolves*. New York: DK, 2003. Read about everything from serpents to sea monsters, Bigfoot to fairies, and vampires to witches in this information-packed volume.

Mihai Spariosu and Dezso Benedek, *Ghosts, Vampires, and Werewolves: Eerie Tales from Transylvania*. New York: Orchard Books, 1994. This illustrated book includes sixteen classic horror tales from Transylvania, the region renowned as the birthplace of Dracula.

Brad Steiger, *The Werewolf Book: The Encyclopedia of Shape-Shifting Beings*. Detroit: Visible Ink Press, 1999. From movies like *An American Werewolf in London* to the best-selling game Werewolf: The Apocalypse, to folklore and case histories, this book is a guide to all things lycanthropic.

Web Sites

Ghosts of the Prairie (www.prairieghosts.com). This site examines unexplained events in Illinois and beyond. It includes a good section on the Bray Road Beast.

HorrorMasters (www.horrormasters.com). Click on the Horror Library link to access the text of more than 30 werewolf classics.

The Werewolf and Shapeshifter Codex (yaiolani. tripod.com). Written by a self-professed werewolf, this site covers everything a curious person might want to know about modern-day werewolves and the werewolf lifestyle.

Index